$\mathcal{L}$ove
is the most
written about
talked about
laughed about
and
cried about

human emotion.

I once said:
"I will never
write about
love."

And then

I loved.

INTRODUCTION

A twenty-five-year anthology. Goodness.

It doesn't *seem* like twenty-five years. In fact, it doesn't seem as though I'm the person who wrote these at all. In selecting and editing these poems, I treated them as though they were written by another. But then, I was informed early-on that I wasn't the author of "my" poetry.

My favorite poem in this book is one of the first I ever wrote. It was 1967. I was seventeen. It was early morning. I had stayed up all night. It was summer. I was in a coffee shop, the only place open in Allen Park, Michigan, at that hour. (Actually, *nothing* was open in Allen Park. I had to cross the border to neighboring Lincoln Park.) Words entered my head, and I wrote them on the only paper available—a napkin.

I must conquer my loneliness
alone.

I must be happy with myself
or I have
nothing
to offer.

Two halves have
little choice
but to
join,
and yes,
they do
make a
whole.

but two
wholes,
when they coincide...

that is
beauty.

that is
love.

After writing it down, I read it. I was astonished. No one had ever taught me about "conquering my loneliness alone." Where did that idea come from? Besides, I couldn't write that well. And where did the word "coincide" come from? Someone or something other than me had written the poem. It was a gift—not just for me, but for anyone who reads it and likes it.

Although I have not written a poem in several years, the gift of poems continues. When I was editing what I thought was the final draft of this anthology, I wanted to check the wording of a poem. I couldn't find it in any of the published books of poetry, but I remembered an earlier unpublished anthology I had put together. I checked the shelf where such things are supposed to be and, lo, next to my unpublished novel and beneath my unproduced screenplay, was the collection of poetry. It was collected fifteen years ago—my ten-year anthology.

There I found a number of poems that, to the best of my knowledge, have never been published before. I've included the best of these in this collection. The gift of poems continues.

The dedication of that ten-year anthology was

*These are
your poems.
I only
wrote them down.*

This collection of poetry is not every love poem I ever wrote—just the ones that, in my old age (forty-two), I am least embarrassed to show others. This is my "for posterity" collection. All the other books of poetry (and there have been something like fourteen of them) are being taken out of print. No new poetry books are planned. This is it.

I feel a mixture of melancholy, relief and a sense of completion in editing and arranging these poems for the last time. I'm calling it *Come Love With Me & Be My Life* because that's what I called my first book of poetry, twenty-five years ago. (Then, as now, I had to publish it myself.) Of all the poems I wrote down, these are the ones that I "hand down to posterity." I wonder if posterity will give a damn.

Do I give a damn? Sure. They're a part of my life. A few of them I'm proud of. The ones I found truly embarrassing I left out. The rest, well, I don't know. What do you think?

If you like them, they are yours. I only wrote them down.

Peter McWilliams
Los Angeles, California
October, 1991

Love is a rope. Give a man enough rope and he'll

wish he had someone to hang onto.

Other books by the author

I Marry You Because...

The Personal Computer Book

Self-Publishing, Self-Taught

...with John-Roger

*You Can't Afford the Luxury
of a Negative Thought*

*LIFE 101: Everything We Wish We Had Learned
About Life In School—But Didn't*

DO IT! Let's Get Off Our Buts

*Focus on the Positive:
The You Can't Afford the Luxury
of a Negative Thought Workbook*

**...with Melba Colgrove, Ph.D., and Harold
H. Bloomfield, M.D.**

How to Survive the Loss of a Love

*Surviving, Healing & Growing:
The How to Survive the Loss of a Love Workbook*

*This book is available,
complete and unabridged,
on audiocassettes,
read by the author.*

Available at your local bookstore, or by calling

1-800-LIFE-101

Prelude Press

Come Love With Me
& Be My Life:
The Collected Romantic Poetry
of Peter McWilliams

ISBN 0-931580-99-4

Published by
Prelude Press
8159 Santa Monica Boulevard
Los Angeles, California 90046

Cover Design: Paul LeBus
Desktop Publishing: Sara J. Thomas

For a free catalog of Prelude Press titles,
please write to the above address or call

1-800-LIFE-101

*H*ow will it happen?
How will it happen
when I find some
someone to spend
a goodly portion
of my life with?

It must.
I mean, I've been
pre-pairing
so long…

It will happen.
Yes.

I will not dwell on
if, only
how, when, where, whom.

*T*here
you were,
dancing.

I saw only your back first.
Then a hint of your profile.
But even then I knew
my search had found
in you a fulfillment.

The long search.

The search I would abandon,
and then realize the search
included that abandonment.

There
you were,
dancing.

hellohellohellohellohellohellohellohellohello
hellohellohellohellohellohellohellohellohello
hellohellohellohellohellohellohellohellohello
hellohellohellohellohellohellohellohellohello
hellohellohellohellohellohellohellohellohello
hellohellohellohellohellohellohellohellohello
hellohellohellohellohellohellohellohellohello
hellohellohellohellohellohellohellohellohello
hellohellohellohellohellohellohellohellohello
hellohellohellohellohellohellohellohellohello
hellohellohellohellohellohellohellohellohello
hellohellohellohellohellohellohellohellohello
hellohellohellohellohellohellohellohellohello
hellohellohellohellohellohellohellohellohello
hellohellohellohellohellohellohellohellohello
hellohellohellohellohellohellohellohellohello
hellohellohellohellohellohellohellohellohello
hellohellohellohellohellohellohellohellohello
hellohellohellohellohellohellohellohellohello
hellohellohellohellohellohellohellohellohello
hellohellohellohellohellohellohellohellohello
hellohellohellohellohellohellohellohellohello
hellohellohellohellohellohellohellohellohello
hellohellohellohellohellohellohellohellohello
hellohellohellohellohellohellohellohellohello
hellohellohellohellohellohellohellohellohello
hellohellohellohellohellohellohellohellohello
hellohellohellohellohellohellohellohellohello
hellohellohellohellohellohellohellohellohello
hellohellohellohellohellohellohellohellohello
hellohellohellohellohellohellohellohellohello
hellohellohellohellohellohellohellohellohello
hellohellohellohellohellohellohellohellohell

*S*omeday we are going to be lovers.
Maybe married.
At the very least, an affair.

What's your name?

I am not
a total
stranger.

I am a
perfect
stranger.

$\mathcal{A}$m I mad?

Am I remarkably lonely
or remarkably perceptive?

How can I be feeling such caring
and tenderness and devotion?

How can I be feeling this
so soon? How have I lasted
without it so long?

"I feel an affinity for you..."

I guess that's as close
as clever people ever
come to saying
"I love you."

On the first date.

I wanted to
spend the night with you
eat with you
take you to meet my friends
make you one of them
take you to bed
make you one with me
say I love you
hear you say the same
meditate, with your heartbeat as
my mantra.

I wanted the sun,
and a goodly portion of the moon.

All I got was this poem,
which I wanted to be
a happy one.

$\mathcal{B}$oredom
becomes
loneliness

when you
know
what you're
missing.

I am lonely.

You are but bored.

*W*as I
born
to be
alone?

Is there
someone
in the
darkness
asking
the same question?

Are we
each other's
answer?

*I*t is a risk to love.

What if it doesn't
work out?

Ah,
but what if it does?

AM I
TOO MUCH
FOR YOU

or
too
little?

We are such
good friends
you & I.

After being
with you
for only
a little while,

I
no longer
relate to
sadness.

*W*hat's
a
kiss
between
friends?

What is
a
friend
between
kisses?

want me

and let me know

you do

I have been
free
now for
quite some time.

free
from the idea
that I needed
any one
to share with me
the limits of my
existence.

but now
you've
come along,
and I find
the lack of
you turns my
alone
moments into
lonely ones.

ouch:
love.

*T*ake time
to be
sure,

but

be sure
not to
take
too much
time.

*L*ove
(man's first
invention)
is a
wheel
(man's first
practical
invention).

we can either
run around it,

or get on
and

GO.

I would
like you
to like
me

but

I would
love you
to
love me.

Missing you

could turn from

pain
to
pleasure

if only I knew

you

were missing me

too.

I don't want
to build my
life around
you,

but I do want to
include you
in the building
of my life.

*I*f you
love me,
tell me
so.

If you
tell me
love me
so.

I am
in love
with you;

that is

I am in love,

hoping you'll
join me.

*T*his whole life spent
growing and learning and
risking and failing and
succeeding and selecting
and gathering and prepairing.

I had begun to wonder:
What is all this for?

And now comes the answer.

You.

I love...
and
oh.

oh oh oh oh
oh oh oh oh oh oh oh
ohoh
oh oh oh oh oh oh oh oh
oh
oh oh oh
ohohohohohohohohohohho
hohohohohohohohohohohohohoho
hohohohoho
ho ho ho ho ho ho
ho ho ho ho
ho

We've both been kicking
around the universe for
some time now, alone,
and doing all right.

But somewhere in the
back of our hearts
was a tugging
—not a perpetual longing,
but a subtle gnawing—
that we might be better
together than
alone apart;
not too dependent,
not too independent,
but rather like the
baby bear's porridge:
Just Right.

I am
falling faster
than I said
I would
or thought
I could…

And you aren't
helping any.

You're so
comforting
&
creative
&
beautiful
&
full filling…

I am falling.
I will flap my arms
and pretend to be flying.

Help me.
Break my
fall.
Catch me
with your smile.

*I*t's hard
to be soft.

your
imperfections
only draw me
closer to you.

they remind me
that you're
human.

that with humans
I have a chance.

*M*y love is
not
a red red rose;

for red red roses
with today's advanced
methods of cross-
pollination are far
too common.

Find me a flower
that is
beguiling,
whimsical,
lyrical,
many-faceted,
perfectly imperfect,
and
one of a kind.

Give it a
name that
matches its
uniqueness,

and to this
I may dare
to compare
My Love.

help me.

show me that
I can love with
out
fears, frustrations,
falsehoods, hesitations.

show me the
face of
god.

CONFOUNDED QUARTERLY

Like a
savings account,
I grow
in direct proportion
to the
amount of
interest paid.

*I*f the painting
of my life were
the Mona Lisa,

you'd be the smile.

*F*amiliarity
breeds
Consent.

all night long.

laughing.
playing with words
pillows blankets time
each other.

falling in love.
falling asleep.

not making love
until the next
morning and the
birds were singing.

*A*fter well over a year of
not making love (I mean
sex has a quality of
its own, but it's not
making love)
and
After meeting (& loving) you
last night (& this morning)
I guess I should spend
this time in poetry (or
"...this time in rhymes,"
a more poetic phrase, but
with the exception of that
phrase, not very descriptive
of my poetry.)

I enjoy you.

your body.
your life style.
your appreciation of me.
your warmth.
your hesitancy to speak &
your freedom to touch.

In holding you I am held.

*H*ush now.

We'll talk
about the
future
when the
present is
less intense.

$\mathcal{W}$e need new words for love.

I feel love.

Not the Universal sort for
flowers and trees and humanity.

Not the Celestial sort
reserved for God and His helpers.

Not the friendly nor the
motherly nor the brotherly

But the one-to-one, interpersonal,
erotic, oftimes neurotic, infatuatory,
undependable gush of desire

I feel for you.

*C*old outside,
warm inside,
and warmer still
inside our stillness.

Come morning
you & I discovered we
and the snow
had fallen
in love.

Outside
we will build a snowman
and a relationship
and love it
until it melts.

*W*hy do I
think of
Christmas
when I see
a rose?

Is it the
red and the green,
or is it the
love?

you make
flowers
of my
hours.

today
was a
bouquet.

*T*he world outside
is a mirror,
reflecting the

good & bad
joy & sorrow
laughter & tears

within me.

Some people are
difficult mirrors
to look into,

but you…

I look at you
and I see
all the beauty
inside of me.

*D*oes the earth
have a sky
or
does the sky
have an earth?

Does the body
have an aura
or
does the aura
have a body?

Do we have love
or
does love have us?

I've heard a lot
about the dangers of
living beyond one's means.

What worries me, however,
is my current habit of
living beyond my meanings.

the morning dew and
me and you at last at one
in this new haiku.

*I*n our first week together
why did I never say

I Love You?

I had the time
and the inclination
and the environment.

I even had the receptivity,
which is the rarest of all.

Why didn't I?

I want to now,

But this is our week
apart.

And who can express love
in a letter?
It sounds
more like a contract
than a feeling...

Oh, but I do love you.

can you feel it?

all those miles,

can I warm you?

I want to
I want you
I love you
I need you
I miss you
I   you

Hurry.

I have something
important
to tell you
when you
return.

I am
blue.

You are
yellow.

Together
we make
green.

And
green
is my
favorite
color...

until I
love some
one who is
red.

colors are brighter
since you've come to
stay a while.

my heart beats in time
with the universal
song of love.

loneliness…pain…
where are you hiding,
my long-time comrades?

maybe they have gone
where you came from;

they will no doubt
return
when you do.

I sleep for a while.

wake up feeling
so much love
for you.

write a joyous poem.

dial your number.

no answer.

write a painful poem.

and sleep for a while.

I missed you last night.
I missed you this morning.
I meditated.
I no longer miss you.
I love you.

*O*f
one
color
that best
describes
my love,

white

is my
choice,
for
white
encompasses
all
colors,

and
my
love
can
become
any
color
required
or
desired...

the red of passion

the orange of intensity

the yellow of happiness

the green of gentleness

the blue of tenderness

the purple of contentment

the gold of love

and
I am my
love's prism

of you
only God
cares more
than I

*W*hen we are
together,
we are
one.

When we are
apart,
each is
whole.

Let this be our dream.
Let this be our goal.

*L*ove,
no matter what
you feel it for,
is still love.

The object does not
change the emotion.

But the emotion
quite often
changes the object.

*T*he difference between
love and loving

is the difference between
fish and fishing.

*M*aturity
is a very
magical
thing...

Now you see it,
now you don't.

I don't know
how to lose.

That's part of the problem.

I don't know
how to win, either.

That's the other part.

you are not perfect,
My Love.

perfection is of
the gods.

the gods are
to be worshipped.

perfection is
to be worshipped.

imperfection
is of man.

man is to
be loved.

imperfection
is to be loved.

My Love,
you are not perfect.

*T*he longing
The laughing
The loving
The living

The joy
The pain
The sun
The rain

Thank you.

I am in love again.

*E*ven on the
busiest of days,
I think about you
every other thought.

I know
I love you.

I do not know
which one of us
those words scare
most.

is it all right
to love you?

is it
completely and absolutely and totally
all right
to love you
completely and absolutely and totally
?

I am one with another
being,
and another being is one
with me,

and the ultimate outward
expression of my Joy
floods this sheet of paper...

not the words:

the tears.

CURRENT AFFAIRS

Essay Exam

Write a brief essay on each of the following points. Use extra paper if necessary.

1. You.

2. Me.

3. We.

I would rather
be with you
than not
be with you.

I would rather be
healthy and rich
than poor and sick.

Keep
us
in
lust

I have this
great poem on
procrastination—

I'll send it to you
real soon.

As soon as
I write it
down.

I don't know whether
I want you because I love you
or
I love you because I want you.

Which came first,
the chicken
or Colonel Sanders?

I do know that I
love being with you and
I like thinking about you.

My love is with you this day.

*Y*ou inspire me so.

Your innocence and worldliness.
Your presence when you're here
and your letters when you're not.
Your phone calls.
Your support.

I love you for choosing me.
I choose you for loving me.

You are as necessary to me as
water to fish,
air to birds or
clichés to my poetry.

I can't imagine what
I did without you. Oh yes,
I remember: I suffered.

*T*he garden loves the rain
and, yes, this is love.

But the love I want for you
—the love I want to give you—
is the love
the rain
gives
the garden.

Loving is giving freedom.

$\mathcal{L}$ove is

Knowing
&
Growing
&
Showing
&
Sewing
&
Hoeing
&
Glowing
&
Flowing
&
Bestowing

Love is two people rhyming.

*T*he world is good.

I feel whole & directed.

Touch my Joy with me.

I cannot keep
my smiles
in single file.

*T*his poem
is a kiss
for your mind.

$\mathcal{M}$y love and
God's Light
be with you

in all that
you are and
in all that
you do.

$\mathcal{T}$he love
I give you
is secondhand.

I feel it first.

*I*n taking,
I get.

In giving,
I receive.

In being loved,
I am filled full.

In loving,
I am fulfilled.

The greatest gift
is to fill a need
unnoticed.

hold me
very close
tonight.

I
want you
more
than I
want my
life.

much
more.

kiss me.
quickly.

I love you.

*W*hy is it
since I met you,
when I hear
the phrase
"sacred union"
I do not
think of the
Teamsters?

*W*hat we have
joined together,
let no one
put us under.

*C*ommitment
is something
one grows into
and then
grows from.

$\mathcal{Y}$ou teach
me things
I never thought
I knew.

I need to be
cared for;
but,
more importantly,
I need to
care.

Marrying is
saying
"I do"
and God saying
"Yes, you do!"

I love you
because
you are my
miracle.

One
touch
is worth
ten thousand
words.

*W*ith you
at 98.6°

I melt.

turn out the light
and then
turn on the light.

"we haven't
said a
thing for
an hour"

                                        "two"

"we didn't
need to"

                                        "no"

"do we
now?"

can you feel my soul
turn its face to God
and smile as you touch me
so

or maybe it's my heart
smiling at my love for

your soul turning to God
or your heart turning to
love

or your hand turning to
touch my face

facing my love
feeling my God

facing my god
feeling my love feel me
so

two lips
meet
to form
one kiss.

two souls
merge
to form
one love.

and this
union
is a
re-
union
with creation...

*I*f
you will
help me
find as
much
meaning
in my life
as I
have found
in our love,

I know
I shall
never
die.

*W*hat a wonderful
place this is,
loving you.

*S*ometimes
it all seems to fit.

In those moments
I appreciate you
most of all.

As I need you less
I love you more.

*I*n those rare
moments when
all desires
have been fulfilled,

my mind
rests
on only
you.

This,
for me,
is Love.

*S*ome business man I am:

My briefcase contains
The Art of Loving,
Intimate Behavior,
Sonnets from the Portuguese,
This is My Beloved,
The Colors of Love,
The Joy of Sex
and a picture
of you.

*E*very time I do
something wonderful,
I immediately think
of sharing it with you.

you are
sleeping.

I will
not disturb
you.

I will
quietly
crawl in
next to
you,
close my
eyes,

and
enter
your
dream.

No cross words

```
    Y   M
L   O   V   E
    U
```

*I*n loving you
I find fulfillment—

A creative being
being creative.

$\mathcal{Y}$ou
are the nicest
thing I could
ever do for
myself.

*Y*our joy
is my
desire.

Your happiness
my vocation.

your fulfillment
my goal.

*E*veryone sighs at
sunsets and roses.

I sigh at
sunsets and roses
and you.

*I*f the purpose of life is loving,
the purpose of my life is loving
you.

*C*ome,
be with me.
Together we'll discover
the secret spaces of the gods.

*W*hen I am with you I am transformed.
I feel transported to a magical land
of Happiness and Laughter and Sunshine.

Toto, I don't
believe we're
in Kansas anymore.

*G*od loves
our love.

$\mathcal{R}$ow
row
row
romance,

gently down the
stream, merrily,
merrily, merrily,
marry me. life
is but a dream.

*A*ny action
performed before
an altar
can be considered
altering.

*Y*ou are now
part of my life.

In all decisions
you are a consideration.

In all problems
(mostly in terms
of solution)
you are a factor.

In all Joy
you are sharing,
in all sorrow
support.

I love you my friend.

I am a friend to you
My Love.

*F*riends
want to
satisfy
needs.

Lovers
need to
satisfy
wants.

$\mathcal{A}$ FEW FACTS OF LIFE:

Earthquakes level large cities.

Birds lay eggs.

Ice is cold.

An orange is orange.

Dogs bark.

Fire is hot.

Bees fly.

I love you.

Sea water contains salt.

Sharks have sharp teeth.

Flowers grow.

Books are made of paper.

you smile.
I forget where I am.
and it takes me longer
each time to remember again.

I want
the feeling
I have
when I'm
near you
to be
with you
all the time.

I cannot write of my love for you.

I cannot select the proper
words and phrases.

I have lost my discrimination.

Since you,
everything is good.

*G*od
created
all things,

but He took
special care
in crafting
the rose
and you.

I had all but
forgotten
this feeling.
A survival mechanism
at work, no doubt.

Somehow the months
have constructed a
mental image of
painless love.

Ha!

*W*hen there are
joys
I want you for
sharing.

When there are
sorrows
I want you for
comfort.

I guess I'm leaning
on your memory
a little too much.

*O*nce upon a time
—and a very long time
ago it was, too—
I was innocent.

I did not know
what love was.

Pain was when you
fell from a tree.

*P*oint number three of the
car rental contract read:

"The expenses arising from
the accident or damage to
the vehicle must be paid
by the hirer."

and point five said:

"The company will pay for
any damages to the vehicle
under hire."

This was to be symbolic of
Our Golden Trip to Spain.

At the bottom of the contract
was written in bold

In CASE OF TROUBEL *[sic]* PLEASE PHONE 27(

I wish I had kept that number handy.

```
      R
    J E A L O U S Y
C R U E L T Y        B        G O
    C                O        A
    T                R        M
    I N D I F F E R E N C E
    O   N            D        S
P A I N              O
    G                M
    R
    A
    T
    L I E S
    U     O
A   D
L O H E S I T A T I O N
N V A            P
R E S E N T      A
  R E            T
          W H Y
          Y
```

*H*ow long will you stay this time,
I ask.

An unfair question,
you respond.

An unfair answer,
I reply.

saying
good night
you
leave,
sentencing
me to a
bad
one.

Hermann Hesse, from *Steppenwolf:*

"The man of power is ruined
by power, the man of money
by money, the submissive man
by subservience, the pleasure
seeker by pleasure…"

and me,
by love.

*E*xcuse me.

I am currently
afflicted with the world's
number one crippler:
infatuation fixation paralysis,

commonly referred to as
love.

Any spare comfort
you have to give
would be most appreciated,
although my ability to receive
may be temporarily impaired.

Thank you.

I don't know
whether I'm being
tested or
forgotten.

something's
wrong.

*T*o paraphrase
an ancient
Chinese Curse:

May you love an
interesting
person.

come
over
and we will
over
come
that which has
come
over
us

all I need is
someone to
talk to
about
you
but
you
are the
only person
I can really
talk to.
trapped.

pain
is
discovering
there
is
nothing
left
to
discover

will you return my call

or not
?

The Longest Night begins.

*D*o you want love,
or do you just want
someone to drive
loneliness from your life?

Do you want me,
or would anyone do?

Do you want to love in return,
or just respond?

I was not put upon this
earth to test your
reflexes.

*Y*ou like it that I write
poems
about you.

Your ego takes some
perverse pleasure
in them.

You will cause
enough pain to fill
a book, and then
send autographed
copies to your
friends.

pain
is
the
presence
of
your
absence

*M*y needs
destroy
the paths
by which
those needs
could be
full filled

$\mathcal{A}$t first you
thought I was
The Perfect Human Being.

I should have known
that in your eyes
the only way I
could go was
down
hill.

I find
I lost.

*I*t's
dangerous
to leave a
lonely man
alone.

You don't
know what
lies
he'll tell
about you.

Or worse,

what truths.

I'd have a nervous breakdown,
only
I've been through
this too many
times to be
nervous.

A FEW THINGS
YOU LEFT BEHIND
YOU'LL NEVER MISS:

one suitcase, empty.
one paperback, bookmark on page 113.
two sox, one white one black.
one tennis shoe, left.
one record, scratched.
me.
brush, plastic handle, nylon bristles.
one key, lock unknown.
one love poem, incomplete.

this longing
may shorten
my life.

$\mathcal{A}$s soon as I
became aware
of my
addictive personality,
I gave up drugs
(illegal ones),
and I never started
on the legal poisons
like alcohol
or tobacco
or television.

But, fool that I am,
I forgot to give up
the most addictive
thing around—
The Hard Stuff:
Love.

And now it's too late.

I'm hooked for life.

An emotion-mainliner.
A touch-junkie.

A love addict.

I sat evaluating
myself.

I decided
to lie down.

who took the
L out of
Lover?

I want to go back.

Back to the time
when your feelings
for me were so
strong that I was
afraid.

Back to a time
when I received
poems in the mail,
and could call you
and hear a smile.

Back to a time
when we made plans
that, at the time,
were realistic.

I was awakened in the middle
of this night by the pounding
of my heart.

Not since I was four or five
have I been so frightened.

I knew that somewhere,
on the other side of this city,
you had reached another of your
unilateral decisions.

You will call me tomorrow,
or the next day,
and calmly tell me
of yet another portion
of our relationship

no.

*W*ho will say
the final
good bye
first,
and who will
make it last:

me and my pain,
or
you and your fear?

I do all right
alone,
and better
together,
but
I do very poorly
when
semi-
together.

In solitude
I do much,
in love
I do more,
but
in doubt
I only transfer
pain to paper
in gigantic Passion Plays
complete with miracles and martyrs
and crucifixions and resurrections.

Come to stay
or
stay away.

This series of passion poems
is becoming a heavy cross to bare.

good
god
go

*E*xpecting
heaven
is what
hell
is all
about.

$\mathcal{M}$y life has fallen down
around me before
—lots of times,
for lots of reasons—
usually other people.

And most of the time
I was fortunate enough
to have a large lump of
that life hit me on the
head and render me numb
to the pain & desolation
that followed.
And I survived.
And I live to love again.

But this,
this slow erosion from below
—or within—
it's me falling down around my life
because you're still in that life
—but not really.
And you're out of that life
—but not quite.

*W*hy must I
always fall for

chicken shits
on
ego trips?

to love
is to be
vulnerable.

to love
you anymore
is to be
dumb.

$\mathcal{L}$eave me here.
Go away.
Love
will come
another
day.

I will rain
until one
takes my
hand
and offers
sun.

*Y*our kindness is cruel.

People afraid of inflicting
pain are awfully painful
to be around.

A rejection somewhere near
the beginning would have been
easy to take,
but your

no now.
ow.

l
lo
lov
love
love
Love
LOve
LOVe
LOVE
LOVE
LOVe
pain
LOVe
LOVe
Love
pain
LOve
LOve
paiN
Love
love
paIN
love
pAIN
love
PAIN
lov
PAIN
PAIN
lo
PAIN
PAIN
PaIN
In
I
i

---

there's not much left,
and very little's right.

pain
is
loving
an
objecting
object

I felt
I needed you.

I was right.

I treated you
not as good as I could.

I was left.

I thought
I wouldn't miss you much.

I was wrong.

is
romanticism
a
treatable
dis-
ease?

run away
run and run
away
quickly
and do not
look back
ever
for I shall
consider that
encouragement
to follow run
run and run
quickly away
quickly.

iamsorry!

the I-Ching
agrees with
you:

we're through.

Splitting Apart
Ching calls it.

I don't agree,
but I seem to be
out numbered.

I think I'll see
what our
horoscope
says.

$\mathcal{L}$eave my life
quickly,

as quickly as you came.

Give me pain and desolation
as quickly and intensely as
you gave love and lust.

Don't let me
fall   a   part.

Go,
leaving a crumpled me
&
no forwarding address

clouds ingest the moon.

raindrops die with a
splat on concrete causeways.

the floodgates are about to burst.

a banshee howls
over our love.

in my sleep
I dreamed
you called. you said
you were moving back
with your old lover.
you said you thought a
phone call would be the
cleanest way to handle it,
"it" being that we could
never see each other
again, and that I should
understand why.
I moved to wake
myself and found I wasn't
sleeping after all.
my life became
a nightmare.

*T*hursday:
drowning in love

Friday:
drowning in doubt

Saturday:
drowning

Sunday:
God, I can't drag my
self to church this morning.
Please make a house call.

morning.
we wake & snuggle.

afternoon.
a phone call, california beckons.

evening.
the airport, a brutal good(?)bye.

night.
o my god. o my god. o my god.

mourning. again.

I know it was time for us
to part,

but today?

I know I had much pain to
go through,

but tonight

?

the fear that I would
come home one day and
find you gone has turned
into the pain of the
reality.

"What will I do if it happens?"
I would ask myself.

What will I do
now that it
has?

rain.
it
rained.
I
fell.
it
rained.
I
loved.
it
rained.
I
lost.
it
rained.
it
loved.
I
rained.
rain.

*W*hat do I do
now that you're gone?

Well, when there's
nothing else going on,
which is quite often,
I sit in a corner and
I cry
until I am
too numbed
to feel.

Paralyzed, motionless
for awhile, nothing
moving
inside or out.

Then I think
how much I miss you.

Then I feel
fear
pain
loneliness
desolation.

Then
I cry
until I am
too numbed
to feel.

Interesting pastime.

and
the
tears
suddenly
turned to
laughter.

"What
the hell
am I
doing
to myself?"

"For
why?

For
who?

For
what?

what?

why?

me...
...alone?"

and the
laughter
returned
to tears.

I found
in you
a home.

Your departure
left me a
Shelterless Victim
of a
Major Disaster.

I called the
Red Cross,
but they
refused to
send over
a nurse.

there is nothing to be
done.

only accept it...

and hurt.

*L*ove
is indeed
that
fabled, clichéd
roller coaster.

I have written
poems of its
ups
and of its
downs...

But what
words can
I use to
describe the
total desolation
of being forced
to
get off
?

I must give you up.
I must give you up.
I must give you up.
I must give you up.
I must give you up.
I must give you up.
I must give you up.
I must give you up.
I must give you up.
I must give you up.
I must give you up.
I must give you up.
I must give you up.
I must give you up.
I must give you up.
I must give you up.
I must give you up.
I must survive.
I must give you up.
I must give you up.
I must give you up.
I must give you up.
I must give you up.
I must give you up.

*O*ur love affair
has crash landed.

I am trapped
in the rubble
of gossamer wings.

The Wright brothers
would have been proud
of our flight, but
we live in an age
of moon landings and
space shuttles.
Our flight was pitifully low
and painfully brief.

Endings
make the circumstances
of the beginnings
regrettable.

you came
and made
my house
our home

you left
making
our home
my asylum

*S*pring:
leaves grow.
love grows.

Summer:
love dies.
I drive away,
tears in my eyes.

Bugs commit suicide on my windshield.

Autumn:
leaves fall.
I fall.

Winter:
I die.
I drive away,
nothing in my eyes.

Snowflakes commit suicide on my windshield.

$\mathcal{F}$irst,
I have to get
out
of love with you.

Second,
I have to remember:

don't fall
until you see
the whites
of their
lies.

*P*lans:

Next month:
find something new.

This month:
get over you.

This week:
get you back.

Today:
survive.

*S*eparating
the memory
of yesterday's warmth
from
the reality
of today's rejection
is a difficult
painful
tedious
exacting
but highly necessary task.

You simply no longer love me.
You simply never will.

How complex.

*W*hen I miss by
several light-years
I shrug and I say,

Oh well, it was never
meant to be.

But when I miss
by only a few inches,

God! That hurts.

I hope I heal soon.

I want to enjoy
Autumn.

This season is called
fall
because everything
nature builds
all summer long
falls
apart.

Like our love.

*P*ain
is not so heavy
a burden in
summer.

Walks
through
travelogue scenes
prevent a good
deal of destruction.

And,
even though no one
is there to warm me,
the sun will.

But
Fall just fell,
leaving Winter,
and me,
with no
warmth within
to face
the cold without.

I might just stick
to the sidewalk
and freeze.

188

I was not ready for you,
but you seemed quite ready for me.

trapped in a week.
drained in a month.
deserted in forty days.

forty days. deserted.

Jesus spent forty days
in a desert once.
He was tempted by
the devil.
We are told he resisted temptation.

fortunately
for The Pope
The Archbishop of Canterbury
and Billy Graham
you were not the devil.

Christianity might never have
gotten off the ground.

*Y*esterday was Sunday.
Sundays are always bad.
("Bloody," as they have been aptly described.)

The full moon is Wednesday.
Full moons are always bad.
(Ask Lon Chaney.)

Friday is Good Friday
and, 30 miles from Rome,
the vibrations of all those mourning
worshippers will make it bad.

Sunday is Easter—but it's also
Sunday,
and Sundays are always bad.

as the
memory
of your
light fades
my days grow dark.

my nights are lit with
electric bulbs. I cannot
sleep. I am afraid of the
dark. I am afraid that you
will return and then fade
again. I am afraid that you
will never return. I am
afraid that my next thought
will be of you. I am afraid
that I will run out of poems
before I run out of pain.

I'm past the point of going
quietly insane.

I'm getting quite
noisy about it.

The neighbors must think
I'm mad.

The neighbors, for once,
think right.

*H*ow I
love you and hate you.

How bound I am to you.
How bound I am to break my bondage.

I want to be free!

I want to be able to
enjoy the day again,

and give me back my nights.

to those
who ever
wished
me ill:

this night
your wish
has been
fulfilled.

I must
remember
that
I must
forget.

I must
forget
what I
remember.

to survive.

to forget

the
un
forget
able.

*S*omeday I will
categorize
the
circle of pain
I put myself through
every time I get
hung up in someone.

I'll have a lot of time
to do it, too.

The insomnia's beginning.

the loneliness that makes me long for you. with you comes the pain that makes me long for solitude. with solitude comes the loneliness that makes me long for you. with you comes

I write only
until I cry,
which is why
so few poems
this month
have been
completed.

It's just
that
I

all the goodness
of my life is
gone.

first you,
and with you
joy
love
freedom.

then
colors
music
trees.

even creativity,
which is always
the last to go,
is only making
a token appearance.

I am Joy.
I am everything.
I can do all things but two:

1. forget that I love you.

2. forget that you no longer love me.

life is becoming
less livable.

with each new person I meet
I wonder, is this the day
fate has chosen, or is fate
what I have chosen to get me
through the day?

loving
is the most
creative
force in the universe.

the memory of loving,
the most
destructive.

I remember thinking once
that it would be good
if you left because
then I could get some
Important Things
done.

Since you've left I've done
nothing. nothing
is as important
as you.

I have done it to me again.

No other being has the power
to hurt me as deeply as I do.

It is the "need"

The "need" for love.

I need love because
I am not happy with I;
me is not satisfied with me.

In order to stop this hurting
I must reach a point of
contentment within myself.

And that will take
some reaching.

*H*ow many more times will
tears be my only comfort?

How many times will I see
that the potential is dead,
and that "our" love was
really in my head?

How many more times will
I give up,

and how many times will I
want you so bad that nothing
seems good?

How many times with you?
How many times
with how many
others?

I'm always around, right?

You never need to miss me.
you never need to care.
or try. or love.

I'm always here, regardless.

I have no rights—
and that's wrong.

Damn! It's only when I'm
with you that I have the
strength to say goodbye.
When you're not near, I
need I need I need.

I no longer look forward
to reconciliation
—only freedom.

you left
traces
of your self
all over my room:

a poem scribbled in the
margin of a book.

the corner of a page
turned over in another book.

your smell on my blanket.

where are you tonight?

in whose room are you leaving
traces?

are you perhaps
discovering
the traces of my self
I left on your soul?

I ceremoniously disposed
of all the objects
connected with you.
I thought they were
contaminated.
It did not help.

I'm the one that's contaminated!

*T*he forgetting
is difficult.

The remembering,
worse.

*A*t a critical moment I said:

I would rather you go
and regret your going
than stay
and regret your staying.

Some day,
at critical moments,
I'm going to
learn to keep my mouth
shut.

I know our
time together
is no more.

Then why do
words
come to mind
that call you
back?

Why do I plan
lifetimes
that include
you?

Why do I
torture
myself
with love
I never felt
while you were
here?

I am missing you
far better than
I ever loved you.

$\mathcal{L}$ife has many secrets.

Where you are tonight
is one of them.

Another: Why, really,
did you go.

The world holds many wonders.

You are one of them.

The layers I have put
around the pain of
your going are thin.

I walk softly through
life, adding thickness
each day.

A thought or a feeling
of you cracks the surface.

A call from you
shatters it all.

And I spend that night in death,
and spin the first
layer of life
with the sunrise.

you cannot come into
my life
again.

don't try to enter
my mind with
your eyes.

it won't work.

I am impenetrable.
aloof.
friendly, but distant.
kind, but cold.

this time
you haven't a chance.

and yet,
your ten minute visit
will cause
ten days
of pain.

how hard the forgetting.
how easy the remembering.
how cruel the process
that possesses me.

*S*he asked me if seeing
you was a drain.

Seeing you is not a drain.

It's a sewer.

*M*y friends are still here:

neglected,
rejected
while I gave all my
precious moments
to you.

They're still here!

God bless them.

help me up
my friend.

dust me off.

feed me warmth.

you are comfort.

let me lean on you
until I can stand
alone.

I will stand a little taller then,

and you will be
proud
to have a friend
such as me.

*M*issing your love
with God's so
close at hand.

It seems somehow
a sacrilege...

but I think
God understands.

I was
overcome,
and now
undone.

this September
will be happily remembered

as soon as it can be
fully forgotten.

*I*t will never be the same.
I will never be the same.

You came.
We loved.
You left.

I will survive until I survive.

And one day, I will
find
myself alive again.

And another day,
another's path will
run parallel to mine
—for awhile.

And yet another day,
you will return,
and I will see

It is not the same.

*B*ridges
built to the
sun,

they burn
don't they
?

the sun will rise
in a few minutes.

it's been doing it
—regularly—
for as long as I
can remember.

maybe I should
pin my hopes
on important
—but often
unnoticed—
certainties
like that,

not on such relatively
trivial matters as
whether you will ever
love me.
or not.

When I
create
something
it doesn't
hurt
as much.

Maybe
that's why
God
created me.

*A*lthough my
nature is not to
live by day,

I cannot
tolerate another
night like this.

So,

I will wake up
early
tomorrow morning and
do do do
all day long,

falling asleep
exhausted tomorrow
early evening,
too tired
even for
nightmares.

*T*o lose you as a
love
was painful.

To lose you as a
friend
is equally painful.

But lost you are.

The walls are sooo high,
and that finely honed saber
I had when I began storming
your citadel isn't even
sharp enough to
slash my wrists.

It's not that I don't care.

It's just that I can't
let myself
care any more.

$\mathcal{T}$o give you up.

God!
What bell of freedom
that rings within me.

No more waiting for
letters
phone calls
postcards
that never came.

No more creative energy
wasted
in letters never mailed.

And, after awhile,

no more insomnia,
no more insanity.

Some more happiness,
some more life.

All it took was giving you up.

And that took quite a bit.

I loved,
which was purgatory.

I lost,
which was hell.

and I survived.
Heaven.

I will never have a love
but
I will never realize this.

It's always
you & you & you,
but it's really
me.

I'll try again
and gain again
and die again
and push on into the night,

to be reborn by a
look and a touch,
and to hope again that
this time it will last,
and to know
it will not be the last.

one thing I forgot:

after the
pain of parting
comes the
happiness of healing;

rediscovering
life,
friends,
self.

Joy.

$\mathcal{A}$ new morning
of a
new life
without you.

So?

There will be others.
much finer,
much mine-er.

And until then,
there is me.

And because I treated
you
well,
I like me better.

Also, the sun rises.

I shall miss loving you.

I shall miss the
Comfort
of your embrace.

I shall miss the
Loneliness
of waiting for your
calls that never came.

I shall miss the Joy
of our comings,
and Pain
of your goings.

and,
after a time,
I shall miss

missing
loving
you.

and
through
all the tears
and the
sadness
and the
pain
comes the
one thought
that can
make
me internally
smile again:

I
have
loved.

Sifting through the
ashes of our relationship,

I find many things
to be grateful for.

I can say "thank you" for
warm mornings,
cold protein drinks,
and all the love you have ever offered
another.

I can say "thank you"
for being there,
willing to be shared.

I can say "thank you" for
the countless poems you were
the inspiration for and the
many changes you were
catalyst to.

But how, in my grasp of
the English language,
faltering as it is,
can I ever

thank you
for
Beethoven
?

$\mathcal{Y}$ou were the best of loves,
you were the worst of loves...

and you left behind several
unintended gifts:

Through you I re-examined my
need (uh, desire?) for one significant
other to share my life.

You commanded in me an unwilling
(but probably much-needed)
re-evaluation of self, behavior patterns,
relationshipping, and a corresponding
change in attitudes;
i.e. growth.

I'm nicer to people.

I'm more in touch with my feelings,
the things and people around me, life.

And, of course, a scattering of poems
(the best of poems, the worst of poems)
that never would have happened
without your disruptions.

Thanks.

$\mathcal{T}$he need you
grew
still remains.

But less and less
you seem to be the way
to fill that need.

I am.

*I*t's been two years
since we talked last.

You lead a church choir
somewhere.

The pauses between your
sentences are longer.
More pregnant—or so
you would like the world
to believe. They make me
as uncomfortable as
ever.

"A person out of the past"
you keep saying, unwilling
to accept my present.

Questions answered by questions.
Statements questioned by silence.

Your ambiguity and my ambivalence
clash again,
for the last time.

the last day of my
loving you is
at hand.

in hand,
a pen, writing one of
the last poems
exclusively yours.

my pain fades,
as autumn did.

winter is too intense
a season to miss
someone in.

the last leaf
fell today.

the first snow
falls tonight.

*C*olor
me
healed.

*P*erfect joy and
perfect sorrow.

One following another,
following another.

The poles—the extremes—
of emotional life, and
all points in between.

Following one another.
Following one another.

Gently up, gently down,
like the ocean under a boat.

$\mathcal{T}$he difference between
"a1one"
and
"a11 one"
is
1
(me),

and a little space.

*L*ife is
not a
struggle.

It's a
wiggle.

I am
the nicest
thing I could
ever do for
myself.

*T*he cosmic dance
to celestial melodies—

free form within
patterns of precise
limitations.

The painting I know
so well. The canvas
I want to learn,

and, perhaps,
someday,
the Artist.

I am worthy.

I am worthy of my life and
all the good that is in it.

I am worthy of
my friends and their friendship.

I am worthy of spacious skies, amber waves
of grain and purple mountain majesties
above the fruited plain. (I am worthy, too,
of the fruited plain.)

I am worthy of a degree of happiness
that could only be referred to as
"sinful" in less-enlightened times.

I am worthy of creativity,
sensitivity and appreciation.

I am worthy of peace of mind, peace on Earth,
peace in the valley and a piece of the action.

I am worthy of God's presence in my life.

I am worthy
of my love.

I must conquer my loneliness

alone.

I must be happy with myself
or I have
nothing
to offer.

Two halves have
little choice
but to
join,
and yes,
they do
make a
whole.

but two
wholes,
when they coincide...

that is
beauty.

that is
love.

Index to First Lines